tammy
T.M.

and Her Family of Dolls

Identification & Price Guide

by John Axe

Hobby House Press, Inc.
Published by Grantsville, MD 21536

cated to Marge Meisinger, a generous and a true friend.

Acknowledgments

ability to complete this project is in direct proportion to the generosity of the following persons: Trudy Banks, Dorothy S. Coleman, Evelyn Jane Coleman, Judy Curtis, Donna Felger, Kimberly Felger, Patricia Gardner, Lee Jenkins, Judy Meisinger, Marge Meisinger, Ted Menten, Dori O'Melia, Sadie O'Neill, Gary R. Ruddell, Richard Rusnock, Betty Shriver, Betty Ann Snider, Phillip M. Snider, Naomi C. Stroup, and Mary Stuecher.

Barbara L. Gilland coordinated the Price Guide and her work is greatly appreciated.

The courtesy of the following was also invaluable: Eddie Brandt's Saturday Matinee, J.C. Penney Company, Inc.; Montgomery Ward and Co., Inc.; *Playthings*; Sears, Roebuck and Co.; and *Toys and Novelties*.

Front Cover: Tammy from 1963.
Title Page: Tammy and Her Family from 1963. From left to right they are Tammy, Pepper, Dad, Ted, and Mom.

Back Cover: Tammy and Her Family of dolls from the second Style Book.

Table of Contents

Preface

In the mid 1970s I researched some of my favorite dolls of all time. These findings prompted my writing *Tammy and Dolls You Love to Dress* (1979). Today the Tammy Family of Dolls is more than 30 years old and a whole new generation of collectors is searching for them. In the past year or so I received more mail pertaining to Tammy than any other subject, so I decided to provide collectors with this revised edition of the original Tammy book.

This new book, *Tammy and Her Family of Dolls*, contains additional Tammy collectibles, such as the long playing records and the book-like savings bank. Hundreds of different Tammy things are pictured and the Price Guide illustrates how the values of Tammy dolls and other collectibles have dramatically increased. In 1979 a Mint-in-Box Tammy was valued at $20.00; now she sells for $50.00 and up. The prices of the other dolls in Tammy's Family have risen as well.

There is a wide range of prices given for each doll, or other collectible, because of the various states of preservation in which they now may be found. A played-with doll in poor condition is always less valuable than one that has been kept in perfect shape. A doll that was produced in limited quantities has risen even more in price, or value, than the more common ones because of its scarcity. Prices have been gathered from doll and collectible shows, from dealers and collectors who know what they pay for their acquisitions. All the Tammy collectibles will continue to rise in value as they become more and more difficult to locate.

Like all good collectibles and things worth saving, Tammy dolls require some special conservation measures. The dolls are made of vinyl, a medium that demands protection and sensible display. It is best not to expose the dolls to direct sunlight or a dusty or smoky atmosphere, as this can fade or darken their coloring and their costumes.

It is imperative that vinyl dolls not come into direct contact with "hard plastic," as the two substances form a chemical reaction and "melt" each other. For example, plastic glasses on the face of a vinyl doll will become "glued" to the doll and both will be ruined in a few years. It is also important to consider the doll's packaging. Tammy and Misty dolls, which were originally sold in a plastic phone booth, should be isolated from their booths, as the plastic that touches the doll will melt. This can be prevented with such simple steps as placing tissue, or fabric, between the two sources.

A good cleaning tip is that a vinyl doll can be cleaned with any substance that is packaged in a vinyl bottle, such as Fantastic. Plastic parts can be cleaned with any substance that is packaged in a vinyl or plastic bottle, regardless of how strong it is. Take precaution, however, to clean your dolls so as not to remove the original paint on faces. Sometimes a strong chemical cleaner will dissolve the paint along with the dirt. Clean vinyl doll faces with a mild soap solution, and rooted hair with "gentle" shampoos. Hair should not be set with substances containing alcohol or oils, as they can cause staining to the vinyl faces and the clothing.

A vinyl doll's worst enemy is the ink from ballpoint pens. Some collectors have recipes for erasing ink and paint remover can also help, but a doll that is badly marked up with ink is probably one who will wear her "tattoos" forever, even if they can be lightened somewhat.

Not all collectors can locate a "needed" doll that is in perfect condition, so compromises are often made in this regard. The best advice I can give when trying to restore a doll is to only clean away dirt and wash the clothing; permanent repainting, re-wigging and part replacement never adds to the value of a doll or any other collectible.

As you add to your collection of Tammy and Her Family of Dolls, remember this: It is better to have a doll that is not perfect than not to have one at all. And, keep your eye out for Patti, which I consider one of the cutest dolls ever made.

Introduction

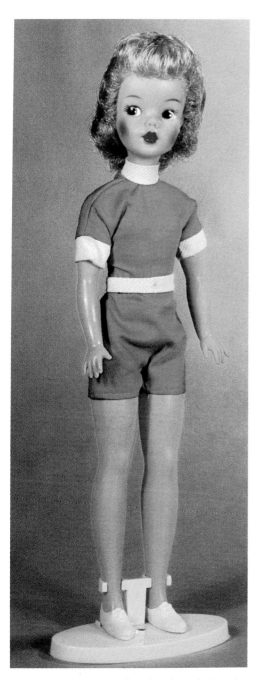

The first Tammy, wearing the playsuit that she came in when she was introduced in 1962. The plastic stand that grips her legs at the ankles came with the earlier boxed sets.

In 1962 The Ideal Toy Corporation introduced one of the most charming modern dolls ever produced. This was the first Tammy - "the doll you love to dress." The obvious comparison must be made: Tammy was Ideal's response to the most successful doll of all time — Mattel's Barbie®, who came out in 1959. Barbie, the $11^1/2$in teen-age fashion doll with a mature figure, changed doll producers' concept of play dolls, and the public's as well. But there was a difference. The early Barbie looked like an international sophisticate. The same-size Tammy always looked like a sweet teenager.

Tammy's name was well chosen. By 1962 the name "Tammy" was already synonymous with sweetness and innocence because of the tremendously popular motion picture *Tammy and the Bachelor* made by Universal-International in 1957. Tammy was played by Debbie Reynolds, the then-epitome of young innocence. The title song from the picture was also a huge hit by the Ames Brothers and later by Debbie Reynolds. Sandra Dee played Tammy in two subsequent films, *Tammy Tell Me True* (1961) and *Tammy and the Doctor* (1963). In 1967 Debbie Watson played Tammy (in which Tammy's last name was changed from Tyree to Tarleton) in *Tammy and the Millionaire*, made from effectively pieced-together television shows. The Tammy films were released by Universal-International and were all based on the novels of Sid Ricketts Summer.

By 1963 Tammy had a "family" of dolls, including Mom, Dad, brother Ted and little sister Pepper. The first Tammy had been introduced with a ready-made wardrobe that was now expanded to include outfits for her family. In the same year the Tammy line was further supplemented with all sorts of accessories, like a car, furniture, a house, carrying cases and other items. In 1964 Tammy, Pepper and Ted were available in "Pos'n" versions with wire inside the vinyl legs and arms so that they could assume various natural positions. In 1964 Tammy also gained a little brother named Pete and Montgomery Ward introduced a "friend" for Pepper named Patti (also made by Ideal).

In 1965 Tammy had a new head and a slimmer body, called the "Grown Up" version and the "New Pepper" was also slimmer. The same year more additions were made to the "family." Tammy now had a friend, Misty, and a boyfriend, Bud. Pepper was joined by her "best friend" Dodi and by Salty, another friend (Pete in a different outfit with baseball equipment). By 1966 Ideal was no longer advertising the Tammy line in the trade magazines (*Toys and Novelties, Playthings*) and catalog sources (Sears, Wards, etc.) no longer carried the dolls. In May of that year the Tammy doll, which originally sold for $1.97 to $3.00, was reduced to as low as 69 cents by Korvette's department stores in the Washington, D.C. area.

Debbie Reynolds and Leslie Nielsen as *Tammy and the Bachelor*, 1957.

Ideal sold thousands and thousands of the Tammy dolls during the short time that she was in production. Tammy was one of the first dolls to be extensively advertised on television. By January of 1964 Ideal had signed a long-term contract with Hanna-Barbera Productions, creators of Yogi Bear, Huckleberry Hound, the Flintstones and others, to produce Saturday children's shows that would advertise Ideal's products. Tammy was advertised on national television 52 weeks a year in such programs as the "Magilla Gorilla Show," an animated cartoon, and the "Peter Potamus Show," another 30 minute cartoon about the global adventures of a purple hippo. Contests were also held to locate little girls who were "Tammy Look-Alikes."

Tammy was distributed in Canada by Ideal's Canadian branch. The leading Canadian doll company, Reliable, also made a Tammy under license from Ideal. In Italy, in September of 1964, Tammy became the first American doll to benefit from mass promotion, including national coverage on television commercials. She quickly became the most popular "fashion doll" in Italy, beating out the competition of the other $11^1/_2$in to 12in teen dolls.

A sure sign of Tammy's success was the speed with which other doll companies put out similar dolls. Eegee, Horsman, and others quickly made equivalent models, including other family members for their basic doll. Pedigree, an English company, introduced its Sindy in 1963. Sindy was very much "suggested by" Tammy and, like Tammy, was followed by other family members. Marx Toys, an American company, began distributing its Sindy under license from Pedigree in 1978, and added a black doll, "Sindy's Friend," to its line.

As the prices of antique and collectible dolls soar, the Tammy line of "modern dolls" (dolls that are about 25 years old) continues to gain in popularity with collectors.

The extensive range of accessories, including clothing, and all the other playthings with the Tammy logo on them also add to the collectibility of Tammy and Her Family of Dolls.

Tammy and Her Family
Tammy

YEAR	STOCK NUMBER	DOLL	SIZE	DESCRIPTION	MARKS
1962	9000-1	TAMMY	12in	vinyl head & arms; plastic legs & torso; head joined at neck base	Head: © IDEAL TOY CORP. BS—12 Back: © IDEAL TOY CORP. BS—12 1
1964	9005-0	POS'N TAMMY	12in	vinyl head, arms & legs; plastic torso; head joined at neck base	Head: © IDEAL TOY CORP. BS—12 Back: © IDEAL TOY CORP. BS—12 2
1965	9100-9	GROWN-UP TAMMY	11¾in	vinyl head & arms; plastic legs & torso; head joined at neck top	Head: © 1964 IDEAL TOY CORP. T—12—E Right hip: © 1965 IDEAL T—12
1965	9102-5	BLACK TAMMY (Dark Grown-Up Tammy)	11¾in	vinyl head & arms; plastic legs & torso; head joined at neck top	Head: © 1964 IDEAL TOY CORP. T—12—E Right hip: © 1965 IDEAL T—12
1965	9105-8	GROWN-UP POS'N TAMMY	12in	vinyl head, arms & legs; plastic torso; head joined at neck top	Head: © 1964 IDEAL TOY CORP. T—12—E Right hip: © 1965 IDEAL T—12

Tammy, Grown-Up Pos'n Tammy and Pos'n Tammy. Note the manner in which the head attachment and leg construction differs for these three versions of Tammy.

Tammy

The box top for the original Tammy. The early Tammys usually had various shades of blonde rooted hair in a short style and painted blue eyes. In the original box there was a always a "Style Book" that showed fashions for Tammy and her family. (See page 9 for the two different booklets.)

Dark-haired Tammy

8

Above: The Style Book that came in the Tammy clothing packages in 1962. Right: The booklet that came with Tammy doll and clothing packages from 1963 and later. These booklets include drawings of the fashions available for Tammy and her family. Some of the illustrations are shown on pages 46, 50, 52, and 74.

Black Grown-Up Tammy.

NEW POS'N
TAMMY

THEY BEN
BIG ACTION IN S

Pos'n Tammy and Pos'n Pep
panion dolls that pose! An add
both dolls have extra long h
styling. Pos'n Tammy even co

Pos'n Tammy from a *Play-things* advertisement by Ideal, August 1964.

MISTY

Tammy's sophisticated, stylish friend. She wears all of Tammy's clothes and uses makeup, too.

TAMMY®

She's all grown up and more beautiful than ever. Gorgeous wardrobe. Each outfit comes complete with makeup for every occasion.

Misty and Grown-Up Tammy, an advertisement in *Playthings*, September 1965.

Black Tammy in her original box is a Grown-Up Tammy, as is the Tammy standing next to her original box (pictured below). These dolls came with wire stands that had a plastic band gripping the doll around the waist. Black Tammy has painted brown eyes and dark brown hair. Note that these dolls were billed as "the teen-age doll you love to dress" on the packaging.

Pos'n Tammy and her Telephone Booth are No. 9105-8 from Ideal in 1965. The backs of the plastic phone booths are also marked: © 1965//IDEAL TOY CORP.//CM-3471. Both of the sets are completely original as they came from the factory. The doll on the left is the Grown-Up Version of Pos'n Tammy from 1965. The doll on the right is the earlier version of Pos'n Tammy from 1964. This is an example of a doll company utilizing remaining stock, as she is dressed in the outfit that the 1965 doll wore. (See page 31 for an original catalog ad for the phone booth.)

Pos'n Grown-Up Tammy

Reliable, Canada, Tammy

Tammy's Dad

YEAR	STOCK NUMBER	SIZE	DESCRIPTION	MARKS
1963	9396-3	13in	vinyl head & arms; plastic legs & torso; head joined at neck base	Head: © IDEAL TOY CORP. M—13 2 Back: © IDEAL TOY CORP. B—12-1/2

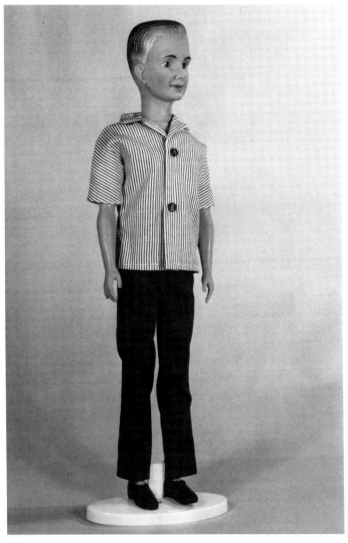

Tammy's Dad

Tammy's Dad has brown painted eyes and brown sprayed hair. Dad came dressed in a red stripped sport shirt and navy slacks. His box lid is shown at the right.

Tammy's Mom

YEAR	STOCK NUMBER	SIZE	DESCRIPTION	MARKS
1963	9395-5	12½in	vinyl head & arms; plastic legs & torso; head joined at neck base	Head: © IDEAL TOY CORP. W—13—L Back: © IDEAL TOY CORP. W—13

Tammy's Mom wears a "French twist," a popular hair style of the early 1960s. Her original box lid is pictured above.

Tammy's Brother Ted

YEAR	STOCK NUMBER	DOLL	SIZE	DESCRIPTION	MARKS
1963	9450-8	TED	12½in	vinyl head & arms; plastic legs & torso; head joined at neck base	Head: © IDEAL TOY CORP. B—12-1/2—W—2 Back: © IDEAL TOY CORP. B—12-1/2
1964	9454-0	POS'N TED	12½in	vinyl head, arms & legs; plastic torso; head joined at neck base	Head: © IDEAL TOY CORP. B—12-1/2—W—2 Back: © IDEAL TOY CORP. B—12-1/2 2

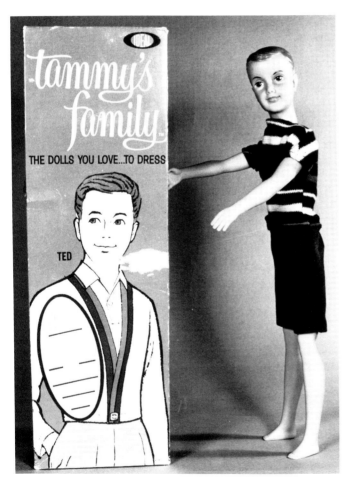

Ted has brown painted eyes and light brown sprayed hair. In the original box he wore a boatneck tee shirt and Bermuda shorts. He was also packed with a plastic stand and a "Style Book." This is the Ted shown on the opposite page. At the left is Pos'n Ted with his original box from the *Lee Jenkins Collection*. The head mold is the same as the regular Ted but the arms are different. They are like the arms on Bud, shown on page 20.

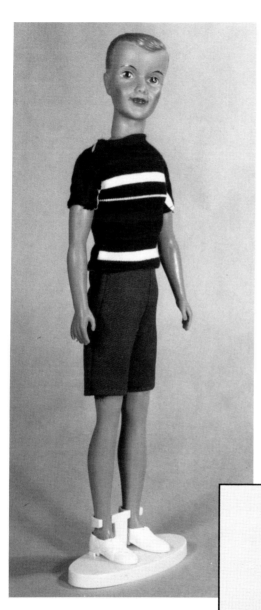

19

Tammy's Boyfriend Bud

YEAR	STOCK NUMBER	SIZE	DESCRIPTION	MARKS
1964	unknown	12½in	vinyl head & arms; plastic legs and torso; head joined at neck base	Head: © 1964 IDEAL TOY CORP. T8 12—W—2 Back: © IDEAL TOY CORP. B 12-1/2 2
NOTE: (The numbers on Bud's back are a larger size than those on Ted.)				

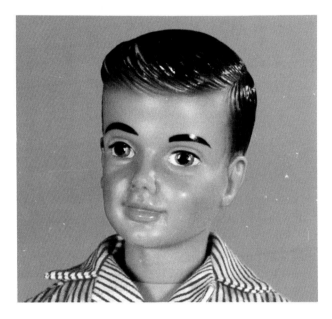

Bud's clothing in the picture at the left is labeled "Tammy's Family" and is the same outfit that Dad is wearing on page 14. It is impossible to determine if it is original to the doll. Bud, the rarest of all the Tammy family of dolls, is from the *Lee Jenkins Collection.* The advertisement shown is from *Toys and Novelties*, August 1, 1965.

Tammy, the fashion doll, is pictured with Misty and Bud. Both girls stand 11½" high and have a complete wardrobe. Bud also has a wardrobe ranging from beach wear to a dress suit. The dolls are made of plastic and have fully jointed arms and legs. Ideal Toy Corp., 200 Fifth Ave., New York City.

Pepper

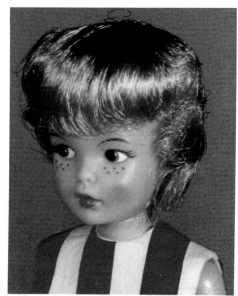

New Pepper

Above: The original Pepper wearing the playsuit in which she was packaged.
Left: The box for the basic 1963 Pepper shown on the title page.

Tammy's Little Sister Pepper

YEAR	STOCK NUMBER	DOLL	SIZE	DESCRIPTION	MARKS
1963	9400-3	PEPPER	9¼in	vinyl head & arms; plastic legs & torso; head joined at neck base	Head: © IDEAL TOY CORP. G9—E Back: © IDEAL TOY CORP. G—9—W 1
1964	9400-3	PEPPER	9¼in	vinyl head, arms & legs; plastic torso; head joined at neck base	Head: © IDEAL TOY CORP. G9—E Back: © IDEAL TOY CORP. G—9—W 4
1964	9405-2	POS'N PEPPER	9¼in	vinyl head, arms & legs; plastic torso; head joined at neck base	Head: © IDEAL TOY CORP. G9—E Back: IDEAL TOY CORP. G—9—W 1
1965	9350-0	NEW PEPPER	9¼in	vinyl head & arms; plastic legs & torso; head joined at neck top	Head: © 1965 IDEAL TOY CORP. P9—3 Right Hip: 1964© (IDEAL) 2 DO—9
1965	9355-9	NEW POS'N PEPPER	9¼in	vinyl head, arms & legs; plastic torso; head joined at neck top	Head: © 1965 IDEAL TOY CORP. P9—3 Right Hip: 1964© (IDEAL) 2 DO—9

Left: Pepper, 1963

Right: New Pepper, 1965

NEW POS'N
PEPPER

POSE! THEY SELL!
WITH SMALL PRICE TAGS!

ers. All the wonderful Tammy and Pepper outfits fit
the Pos'n dolls. See-thru pacs show off the posing
feature and sell themselves. Pos'n Tammy and Pos'n
Pepper will be on national TV 52 weeks a year.

IDEAL

Ideal Toy Corp., 200 Fifth Ave. N.Y. 22, N.

The advertisement at the left is from
Playthings, August 1964 and is for
Pos'n Pepper. The doll, above, also
shown with her original box, is actually "New Pos'n Pepper" from
1965. She is wearing a navy blue and
white playsuit. The swing is cardboard with red cord and was attached to the original package. All
the Peppers have blue painted eyes
and rooted hair of various shades,
usually blonde. Pepper also has
freckles across her nose.

Pepper's Friend Dodi

YEAR	STOCK NUMBER	DOLL	SIZE	DESCRIPTION	MARKS
1964	9300-5	DODI	9in	vinyl head & arms; plastic legs & torso; head joined at neck top	Head: © 1964 IDEAL TOY CORP. DO—9—E Right Hip: 1964© (IDEAL) 1 DO—9
1965	?	POS'N DODI	9in	vinyl head, arms & legs; plastic torso; head joined at neck top	Head: © 1964 IDEAL TOY CORP. DO—9—E Right Hip: 1964© (IDEAL) 1 DO—9 or 2 DO—9

The 1964 Dodi. She has rooted hair of various shades and has the same body as New Pepper. Pos'n Dodi, 1965, like all the "Pos'n" dolls, has bendable wires inside the legs and arms for flexing into different positions.

Dodi

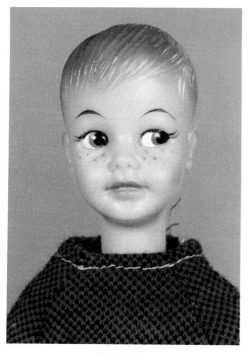

Pos'n Pete

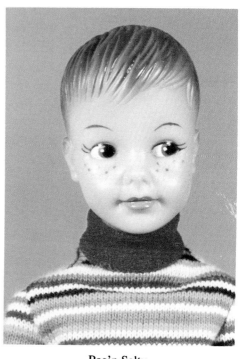

Pos'n Salty

Pos'n Pete

YEAR	STOCK NUMBER	SIZE	DESCRIPTION	MARKS	
1964	9449-0	7¾in	vinyl head, arms & legs; plastic torso; head joined at neck base	Head:	© 1964 IDEAL TOY CORP.
				Back:	© 1964 IDEAL TOY CORP. P—8

The same doll was used for Pete, Tammy's Little Brother, and Salty, Pepper's Friend. The difference is in the clothing. Shown above is Pos'n Pete with his original box. Both Pete and Salty have brown painted eyes and sprayed brown hair and are freckled like Pepper. Both Pete and Salty are difficult to find in original condition.

Pepper's Friend Pos'n Salty

YEAR	STOCK NUMBER	SIZE	DESCRIPTION	MARKS
1965	9448-2	7¾in	vinyl head, arms & legs; plastic torso; head joined at neck base	Head: © 1964 IDEAL TOY CORP. Back: © 1964 IDEAL TOY CORP. P—8

Salty, 1965.

27

Pepper's Playmate Patti

YEAR	STOCK NUMBER	SIZE	DESCRIPTION	MARKS
1964	8318	9¼in	vinyl head & arms; plastic legs & torso; head joined at neck base	Head: © IDEAL TOY CORP. G9—L Back: © IDEAL TOY CORP. G—9—W 2

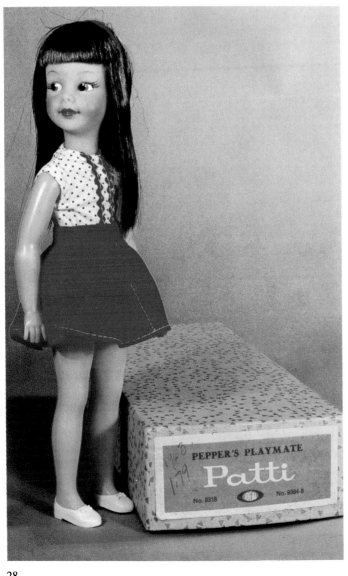

Patti is one of the rarest of all of the Tammy family dolls as she was sold only as a Montgomery Ward exclusive during the Christmas seasons of 1964 and 1965. The body is the same as that used for Pepper. The head is far more realistic and childlike than the other Ideal dolls of Tammy's family. Patti has painted blue eyes and long dark brown rooted hair of a softer texture than any of the other dolls of Tammy's family. In 1964 Montgomery Ward sold Patti and Pepper for $1.74 each. The following year their price was increased by 5 cents.

29

Glamour Misty the Miss Clairol Doll

YEAR	STOCK NUMBER	SIZE	DESCRIPTION	MARKS
1965	9809-5	12in	vinyl head & arms; plastic legs & torso; head joined at neck top	Head: © 1965 IDEAL TOY CORP. W12—3 Right Hip: © 1965 IDEAL 2 M—12

Glamour Misty, the Miss Clairol Doll, has platinum rooted hair that can be tinted blonde, red or brunette. She has green painted eyes. Her feet are shaped to wear higher heeled shoes than Tammy.

Pert 'n pretty
Pos'n Tammy
$2⁹⁴

Smart, new
Pos'n Misty
$2⁹⁴

Left: Catalog page, Christmas 1965. *Courtesy of Sears, Roebuck and Co.*

Below: Catalog page, Christmas 1965, © J.C. Penney Company, Inc. 1979. Reproduced by permission.

Glamour Misty

Glamour Misty

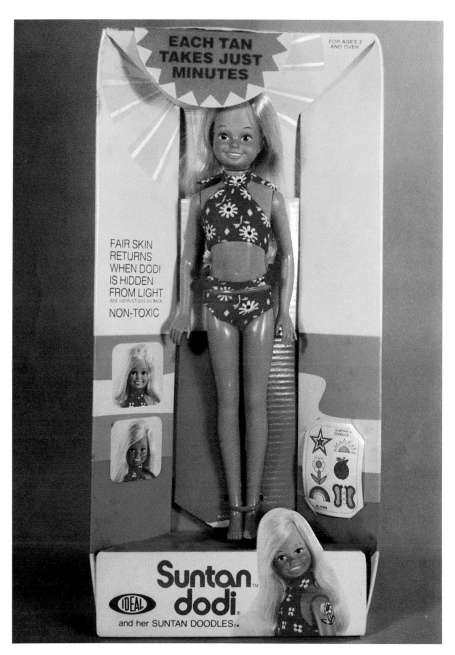

The only "survivor" of the original Tammy family of dolls is Dodi, as she appeared on the market again in 1978. She is Suntan Dodi, part of a series of dolls that includes Suntan Tuesday Taylor and Suntan Eric. The dolls are made from a material that darkens when exposed to direct sunlight and lightens again when removed from the sun, like tinted sunglasses. The head is from the same mold as the original

Dodi, except that the blue eyes look ahead rather than to the side. This doll was made in Hong Kong and the package is copyright 1977.

The head is marked: © 1964
                                         IDEAL TOY CORP.
                                         DO—9—E
The left hip is marked: HONG KONG
The right hip is marked: © 1977 IDEAL
                                       HOLLIS N.Y. 11423

Reliable
Made in Canada Tammy

On this page and the opposite one are three different Tammys that were made in Canada by Reliable. The date of manufacture is not known, but the booklet in the original boxes, which is lithographed in Canada, only shows the early Tammy outfits by Ideal. The dolls are from the same mold as Ideal's American Tammy, although the markings are different. The playsuit is the same style also, but it is a darker shade of blue and not quite as well made. The original boxes for the dolls with Ideal logos glued

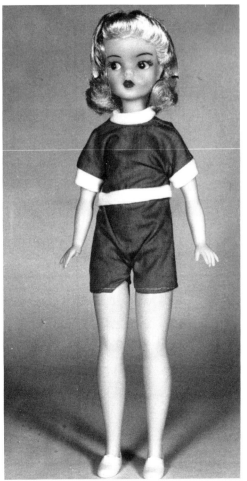

over the Reliable ones, read:

182123
MADE IN CANADA BY
RELIABLE TOY CO. LIMITED
UNDER LICENSE FROM
IDEAL TOY CORPORATION, U.S.A.

The head and the arms of the dolls are vinyl; the legs and the torso are plastic. The eyes are painted blue. The hair on two of the dolls is light blonde and dark red on the other one. The heads are a lighter weight vinyl than on the American Tammys and are marked:

©IDEAL
TOY
CORP

The backs are marked:

CANADA

Ideal Toy Co. of Canada, Limited

POS'N PEPPER			
YEAR	**STOCK NUMBER**	**SIZE**	**MARKS**
1964	9405-2 CAN	9^1/$_4$in	Head: © IDEAL TOY CORP. G9—E Right Hip: © IDEAL TOY CORPORATION MADE IN JAPAN

POS'N TAMMY			
YEAR	**STOCK NUMBER**	**SIZE**	**MARKS**
1965	9005-0 CAN	12in	Head: © IDEAL TOY CORP. BS—12 Back: © IDEAL TOY CORP. BS—12 MADE IN JAPAN

Pos'n Pepper and Pos'n Tammy from Canada by Ideal Toy Co. of Canada, Limited. They are the same basic dolls as the American versions by Ideal except that the boxes and the dolls are marked differently. On the opposite page they are seen in their original boxes and their markings are given in the charts.

Tammy's Little Sister Pepper, "a pre-teen doll just like you!", wearing a blue and white dress from Ideal Toy Co. of Canada, Limited.

The box is marked:

No. 9400-3 CAN: © 1964

The head is marked:

© IDEAL TOY CORP.
G9—E

The back is marked:　　　MADE IN JAPAN.

An article in the March, 1965, *Playthings* showed this page from the Italian equivalent of *Playthings*. "Tammy from America" had "100 vestiti" (100 outfits) and was a great success in 1964 because she was marketed using American-style advertising, merchandising and promotional techniques. The Tammy commercials caused a great sensation in Italy, as this was the first doll ever advertised on television there. Ideal sponsored contests in Italy for store window displays featuring Tammy with the prize being a trip to New York City for the 1965 Toy Fair. The Tammy line in Italy was increased in 1965 to include Pepper, the Pos'n versions of Tammy and Pepper and various accessories like cars, beds and vanity sets. Tammy cornered the Italian doll market and hundreds of thousands of Tammy dolls were sold in Italy.

(Left to right) Pete, Tammy and Pepper
shown for size comparisons.

(Left to right) Pepper, Patti and Dodi
shown for size comparisons.

Fashions for Tammy and Her Family

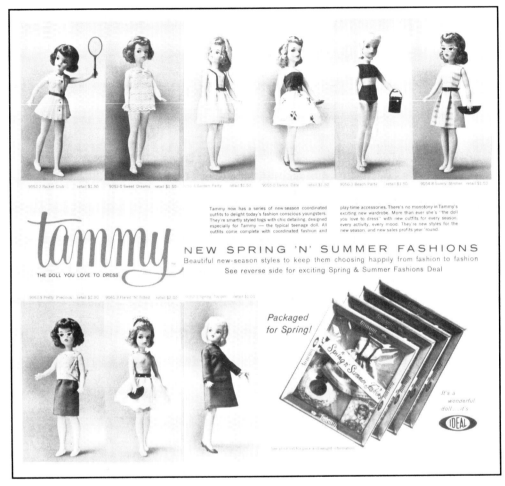

Advertisement in *Playthings*, 1964.

The following pages show the packaged outfits for Tammy and Her Family. The listings give the numbers of the outfits and describe them. If there is a third number in the series, it was the original price of the package; for example, #1997-3-250 sold for $2.50.

Tammy's Boxed Outfits

9051-4-150	Garden Party	dress, picture hat, shoes
9052-2-150	Racket Club	shorts, blouse, shoes, badminton racquet
9053-0-150	Sweet Dreams	shorty pajamas, slippers, glass, mirror, comb, brush
9054-8-150	Sunny Stroller	dress, belts, purse, shoes, sunglasses
9055-5-150	Dance Date	dress, belt, purse, shoes
9056-3-150	Beach Party	two-piece swim suit, cap, sandals, bag
9061-3-200	Flared 'N' Fitted	sheath dress, skirt, shoes, hose, date book
9062-1-200	Spring Topper	coat set
9063-9-200	Pretty Precious	skirt, top, glasses, shoes, news magazine
9091-0-200	Underwear Outfit	sheer petticoat, panties, bra, comb, brush, mirror, sandals
9092-8-200	Sleepytime	shorty pajamas, slippers, comb, curlers, glass of milk
9093-6-200	Fun in the Sun	one-piece bathing suit, cap, poncho, sandals, beach mat
9094-4-200	Knit Knack	crocheted dress and beret, shoes
9111-6-250	Puddle Jumper	raincoat, scarf, boots, umbrella, shoulder bag
9113-2-250	Tennis the Menace	jamaicas, blouse, belt, socks, shoes, sunglasses, tennis racquet, racquet press, head band
9114-0-250	Walking Her Pet	leatherette skirt, plaid top, scarf, gold heart, shoulder bag, shoes, dog
9115-7-250	Pizza Party	harlequin top, leotards, sandals, glasses, news magazine, pizza
9117-3-250	Beau and Arrow	hooded shirt, dungarees, shoes, bow, arrows, target
9118-1-250	Tee Time	panty-blouse, skirt, hat, belt, tees, bag, clubs
9119-9-250	Purl One	dress, hanky, shoes, shoulder bag, knitting bag with wool and needles
9120-7-250	Nurse's Aide	uniform, cap, stethoscope, hypodermic, tongue depressors, clip board
9131-4-250	Cheerleader Outfit	sweater, skirt, cap, socks, sneakers, baton, megaphone
9132-2-300	Cutie Co-ed	jumper, blouse, leotards, carry bag, transistor radio, heart on chain, red sneakers
9133-0-300	School Daze	dress, belt, shoes, typewriter, princess phone, portfolio, phone book
9134-8-300	Picnic Party	skirt, clam digger pants, headband, sneakers, sunglasses, picnic basket, table cloth, transistor radio
9135-5-300	Sweater Girl	red sweater, skirt, necklace, camera, glasses, purse, date book
9136-3	(ballerina)	body suit, skirt, leotards, flowers, slippers, bag
9137-1	Fraternity Hop	sleeveless gown, cape, hose, shoes, purse, necklace, bracelet

(Continued on Page 44.)

9152-0-350	Ring-a-Ding	blouse, pants, wedgies, phone, phone book, plate of fruit, TV set
9153-8-350	Dream Boat	satin and brocade dress and jacket, headband, shoes, purse, date book, camera
9155-3	Jet Set	car coat, plaid pants, kerchief
9168-6	On the Town	velvet, fur-trimmed jacket and dress
9169-4-400	Beauty Queen	gown, long gloves, sash, crown, purse, trophy, bouquet, hairpins, shoes
9172-8-400	Travel Along	shift, belt, kerchief, stockings, pumps, glasses, shoulder bag, hat box, news magazine
9173-6-400	Model Miss	wool coat, cap, shoes, nylons, pocketbook, hat box, bracelet, date book
9174-4-400	Sorority Sweetheart	jerkin, blouse, skirt, stockings, pumps, ribbon, glasses, phone book
9175-1-400	Checkmate	blouse, skirt, blazer, camera, shoulder bag, necklace, hairbow, stockings, shoes
9176-9-400	Fur 'N' Formal	gown, stole, necklace, bracelet, gloves, bag, headband, hose, shoes
9177-7-400	Skate Date	skating dress, panties, nylons, headband, roller skates, shoes, skating bag
9211-4-500	Snow Bunny	ski jacket, pants, boots, mittens, skis, poles
9212-2-500	Figure 8	pants, jacket, scarf, gloves, skates, shoes
9213-0	Wedding Belle	long wedding gown, veil, tiara, fur stole

Tammy's Clothes on Cards

9220-5-80A	sheath skirt, belt, date book, hanger
9221-3-80A	pleated plaid skirt, shoes, hanger
9222-1-80A	sleeveless blouse, shoes, necklace, hanger
9223-9-80A	slacks, sandals, hanger
9224-7-80A	pedal pushers, newspaper, glass, hanger
9230-4-100B	full skirt, heart, hanger
9231-2-100B	short sleeve blouse, glasses, hanger
9232-0-100B	long sleeve blouse, purse, hanger
9233-8-100B	plaid jumper, purse, shoes, hanger
9234-6-100B	sleeveless sweater, glasses, hanger
9240-3-120C	housecoat, phone, hanger
9241-1-120C	sleeveless shirtwaist dress, two belts, hanger
9242-9-120C	shorty nightgown, slippers, fruit, hanger
9243-7-120C	sheath dress, belt, shoes, hanger
9244-5-120C	heavy woolen sweater, scarf, hanger
9245-2-120C	afternoon dress, shoes, hanger

Tammy's Accessories on Cards

(Note: The second set of numbers is the original price.)

9180-80	hose, red shoes, red purse, red belt
9181-80	curlers, comb, brush, mirror, spray net
9182-80	glasses, purse, radio and carrying case, news magazine
9183-80	travel bag, camera, airline ticket
9184-80	phone, directory, pizza, sandals
9185-80	bowl of fruit, TV set, TV guide, news magazine
9186-80	dog, red purse, shoes
9187-80	typewriter, phone directory, date book
9188-80	tennis racquet and frame, ball, shoes, score book
9189-80	purse, belt, scarf, hanky, necklace

Store display rack for Tammy outfits on cards. *Betty Ann Snider Collection. Photograph by Phillip M. Snider.*

PUDDLE JUMPER (≠9111-6)

Let it rain. Tammy can show off her chesterfield raincoat. She protects her hair with the matching scarf. She wears the cutest white boots and carries a red shoulder bag. For heavy downpours, Tammy has her own umbrella. Style book.
Complete set (without doll)
$2.50

DREAM BOAT (≠9153-8)

It's date night and Tammy's going to a party. Her beau will be proud to escort this vision in blue satin and brocade with removable embossed silk jacket. Her pretty flowered headband and dainty shoes will make Tammy look like the queen of the ball. She has a gold purse, date book and camera. Style book.
Complete set (without doll)
$3.50

From the first Tammy Style Book.

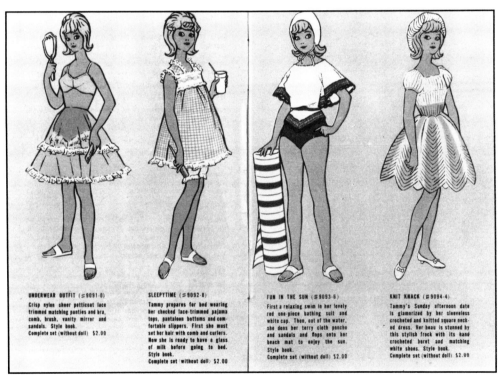

UNDERWEAR OUTFIT (≠9091-0)

Crisp nylon sheer petticoat lace trimmed matching panties and bra, comb, brush, vanity mirror and sandals. Style book.
Complete set (without doll) $2.00

SLEEPYTIME (≠9092-8)

Tammy prepares for bed wearing her checked lace-trimmed pajama tops, pantaloon bottoms and comfortable slippers. First she must set her hair with comb and curlers. Now she is ready to have a glass of milk before going to bed. Style book.
Complete set (without doll) $2.00

FUN IN THE SUN (≠9093-6)

First a relaxing swim in her lovely red one-piece bathing suit and white cap. Then, out of the water, she dons her terry cloth poncho and sandals and flops onto her beach mat to enjoy the sun. Style book.
Complete set (without doll) $2.00

KNIT KNACK (≠9094-4)

Tammy's Sunday afternoon date is glamorized by her sleeveless crocheted and knitted square necked dress. Her beau is stunned by this stylish frock with its hand crocheted beret and matching white shoes. Style book.
Complete set (without doll) $2.00

From the second Tammy Style Book.

Right: #9094-4 *Knit Knack* modeled by the first Tammy. She is wearing the pink and white dress and holding the blue and white one.

#9111-6 *Puddle Jumper.*

#9132-2 *Cutie Co-ed.*

Left: #9114-0 *Walking Her Pet. Courtesy Sears, Roebuck and Company*, 1963 Christmas Catalog.

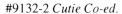
Opposite Page: 9131-4 *Cheerleader* modeled by the first Tammy.

Left: #9117-3 *Beau and Arrow.*

Below: From the second Tammy Style Book.

BEAU AND ARROW (#9117-3)
Tammy has just learned to shoot her bow and arrow. On the archery range she wears a red and white knit shirt with attached hood and dungarees. She's still hoping to hit the bullseye. White sneakers. Style book. Complete set (without doll) $2.50

TEE TIME (#9118-1)
Tammy scores a hole in one as soon as she reaches the first tee in her perky aqua panty-blouse and golf skirt. She has a sun hat and golf belt with three tees. Her caddy carries her plastic golf bag. Sneakers and score card included. Style book. Complete set (without doll) $2.50

PURL ONE (#9119-9)
This tailored sleeveless shirtwaist dress with button down front is perfect for Tammy who loves to socialize while knitting. Red and black shoulder bag, checked hanky, knitting bag with wool, 2 knitting needles and matching shoes complete this outfit. Style book. Complete set (without doll) $2.50

CHEERLEADER OUTFIT (#9131-4)
Tammy leads the school cheers with her megaphone. She's wearing a bulky white sweater with letter T, short red flared felt skirt and matching cap with chin strap. Tammy wears high socks with her white sneakers. She twirls her baton as the stadium roars. Style book. Complete set (without doll) $3.00

#9173-6 *Model Miss.*

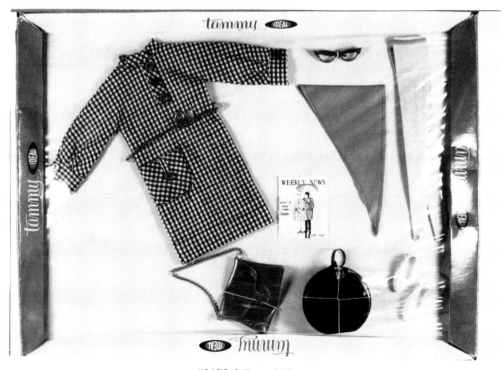

#9172-8 *Travel Along.*

CHECKMATE (≠9175-1)

The girls are going to a matinee.
Tammy will look lovely in her 3-piece
outfit of red checked blouse, white
pleated skirt and blue wool blazer
jacket lined in matching checked
material. With her camera She'll snap
pictures of her friends posing with the
stars of the show. Her accessories
include a shoulder bag, double strand
pearl necklace, hair bow, nylon
stockings and weekly news. White shoes
and style book.
Complete set (without doll) $ 4.00

Left and below: From the first
Tammy Style Book.

SCHOOL DAZE (≠9133-0)

To impress the cute boy in her class,
Tammy wears a dress with a red ribbed
top and full plaid skirt; gold belt
goes around her waist. At home, she
does her homework on her typewriter,
but waits for her boyfriend's call on
her Princess phone. She has her own
phone book. Tammy carries her homework to school in her zippered red
portfolio. Red shoes. Style book.
Complete set (without doll) $ 3.00

SORORITY SWEETHEART (≠9174-4)

Tammy has her sorority emblem on the
white wool jerkin that she wears over
a mix-and-match outfit of long-sleeved
checked cotton blouse and blue wool
pleated skirt. Her outfit is complete
with nylon stockings, red ribbon and
red heeled pumps. After the meeting,
the sorority sisters watch their favorite
shows on Tammy's own portable
TV. They use her phone to call their
friends. Eye glasses, phone directory
and Style book.
Complete set (without doll) $ 4.00

#9177-7 Skate Date modeled by dark-haired Tammy. *Judy Meisinger Collection.*

53

#9211-4 *Snow Bunny.*

#9137 *Fraternity Hop* from the *Betty Ann Snider Collection.*

#9118-1 *Tee Time*.

Left: #9051-4 *Garden Party*.

Above: #9052-2 *Racket Club*.

#9134-8 *Picnic Party.*

#9136-3 *Ballerina* from the *Betty Ann Snider Collection.*

#9120-7 *Nurse's Aide.*

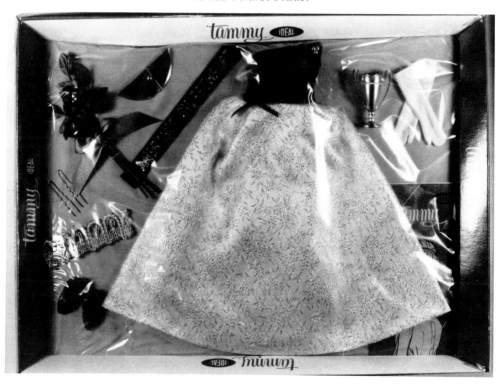

#9169-4 *Beauty Queen.*

Upper Left: #9220-5 blue skirt.

Upper Right: #9221-3 plaid skirt.

Lower Left: #9223-9 plaid slacks.

#9224-7 pedal pushers.   #9233-8 jumper.

All packages from the *Betty Ann Snider Collection.*

#9240-3 house coat.   #9241-1 shirtwaist dress.

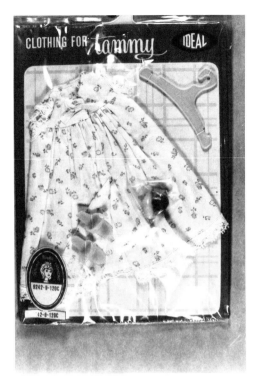

#9242-9 shorty nightgown.   #9243-7 sheath dress.

All packages from the *Betty Ann Snider Collection*.

#9244-5 sweater.   #9245-2 afternoon dress.

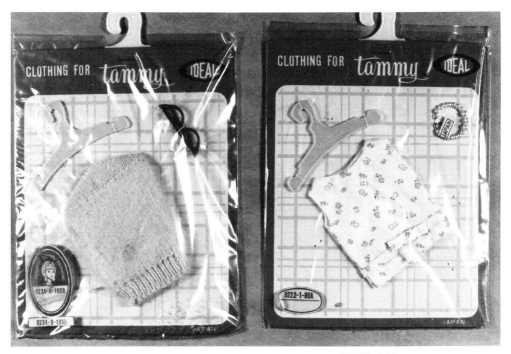

#9234-6 sweater.   #9222-1 blouse.

All packages from the *Betty Ann Snider Collection.*

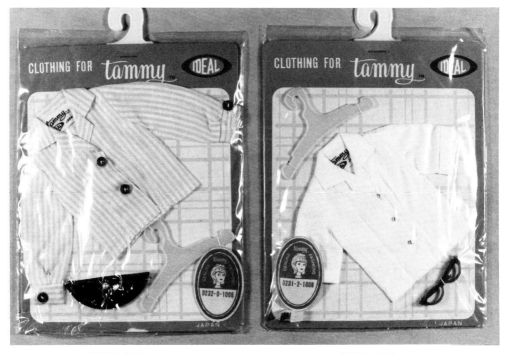

#9232-0 blouse.   #9231-2 blouse.

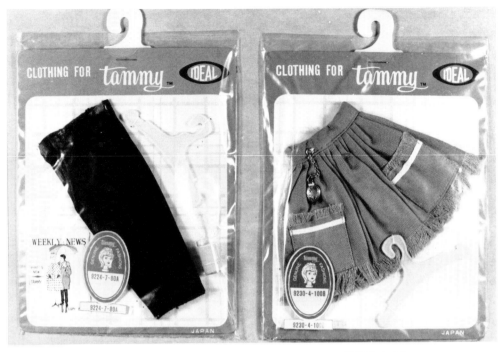

#9224-7 pedal pushers.   #9230-4 skirt.

Betty Ann Snider Collection.

#9180 hose, red shoes.   #9186 Tammy's dog (see also page 48).

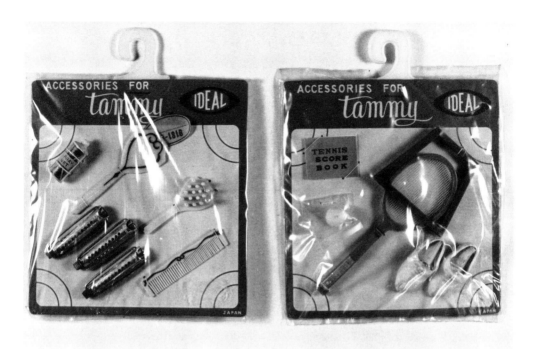

#9181 curler accessories.   #9188 tennis accessories.

All packages from the *Betty Ann Snider Collection.*

#9182 glasses, purse, radio,   #9184 phone, directory, pizza, sandals.
carrying case, news magazine.

#9183 travel bag, camera, airline ticket.   #9187 typewriter, phone, directory, date book.

All packages from the *Betty Ann Snider Collection.*

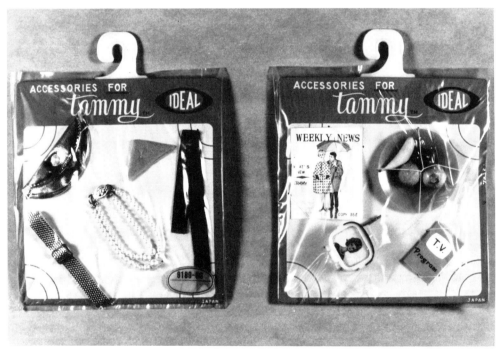

#9189 purse, belt, scarf, hanky, necklace.   #9185 bowl of fruit, TV set,
TV guide, news magazine.

#9062 *Spring Topper* modeled by Grown-Up Tammy.

Canadian Boxed Outfits for Tammy and Misty

#9052 Racket Club. (Compare with the American package on page 55.)

On pages 66-69 are the boxed sets that were sold by Ideal in Canada. The information on the boxes is in both French and English. These outfits are variations of the same ones that were sold in the United States. Instead of accessories, the boxes include a make-up bar, which is colored pencils and rouge with an applicator. For example, the Canadian set #9053 *Sweet Dreams* is the same as the American set #9053-0 *Sweet Dreams* but the make-up bar is substituted for the comb, brush, and mirror. See the list on pages 43 and 44 and match the numbers for the description of what the package should include. Note that on the Canadian sets Misty gets first billing. (The Canadian packages have only a four-digit number.)

some of the dress-up & make-up fashions from (IDEAL) MISTY'S & TAMMY'S large collection

quelques-uns des ensembles et toilettes de la vaste collection pour MISTY et TAMMY

More Tammy and Misty outfits that were shown on the back of the Canadian packages. These are variations of the American Tammy outfits and are all modeled by Glamour Misty.

Glamour Misty wearing #9061-3 *Flared 'N' Fitted.*

#9055 *Dance Date*.

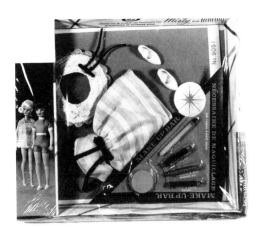

#9051 *Garden Party*.

#9056 *Beach Party*.

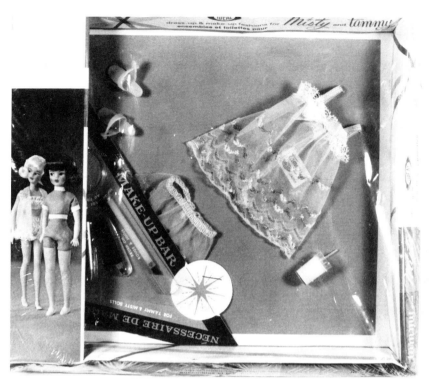

#9053 *Sweet Dreams.*

#9054 *Sunny Stroller.*

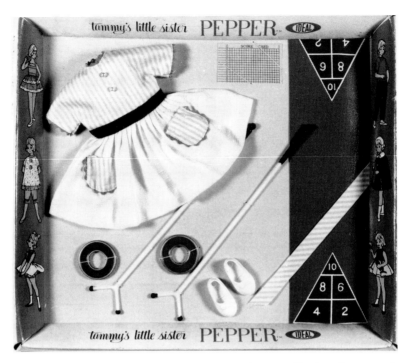

#9317-9 *Happy Holiday. Betty Ann Snider Collection.* (The later boxes read: "Fashions for Tammy's Little Sister Pepper and her friend Dodi.")

Pepper's Boxed Outfits

9306-2	Budding Ballerina	tutu, head piece, ballet shoes, satin bag
9307	(shorty pajamas)	two-piece pajamas, nightcap, comb, brush, mirror, glass, Weekly News
9308-8	Teacher's Pet	dress, shoes, school book, bag, bulletin board, tacks
9317-9	Happy Holiday	dress, headband, shoes, shuffleboard, score pad
9318-7	After School	denim slacks, hooded pullover, shoes, ping pong set
9326-0	Birthday Party	nylon dress, shoes, record player, record rack, records, album
9327-8	Cat's Meow	slacks, cardigan, blouse, shoes, kitten basket, food bowl, catnip
9331-0	Miss Gadabout	velvet skirt, Eaton jacket, blouse, straw hat, shoes, gloves, travel bag, purse, airline ticket, magazine
9332-8	Flower Girl	gown, gloves, tiara, necklace, basket of flowers
9339-3	Snow Flake	snow pants, hooded parka, mittens, boots, sled

#9404-5 *Class Room Caper* from the *Betty Ann Snider Collection.*

Pepper in the basic playsuit, Pepper in #9409-4 *Party Time* and Pepper in #9306-2 *Budding Ballerina.*

Pepper's Clothes on Cards

9401-1-100	Nylon Undies	
9403-7-120	Bed Time	two-piece pajamas, slippers
9404-5-120	Class-Room Caper	dress with flared skirt, panties
9406-0-150	After School Fun	knitted wool sweater, slacks
9408-6-200	Frosty Frolics	flannel coat with fur collar, headband
9409-4-200	Party Time	nylon and velvet dress, matching bag

#9403-7 Bed Time

#9401-1 Nylon Undies

Pos'n Pepper in #9406-0 *After School Fun* and Pepper in #9408-6 *Frosty Frolics*.

#9419-3 *Shopping Topping*.

EVENING IN PARIS (≠9421-9)
Mom goes out formal with Dad in this strapless gold brocade sheath. A black velvet stole and necklace crown her beauty. Style leaflet and gold pouch included.
Complete set (without doll) $2.00

From a black and white folder that came in Tammy's Family clothing on cards.

Mom's Clothes on Cards

9415-1-100	Nighty Nite	nightgown, wedgies, hanger
9417-7-150	Hidden Glamor	lace bra, panty, half slip, hanger
9418-5-150	Lazy Days	brunch coat, hanger
9419-3-150	Shopping Topping	sleeveless dress, hanger
9421-9-200	Evening in Paris	sheath, stole, necklace, hanger
9422-7-200	Lounging Luxury	brocade pants, blouse, wedgies, hanger

All of Mom's clothes on cards are from the *Betty Ann Snider Collection*.

#9415-1 *Nighty Nite.*

#9418-5 *Lazy Days.*

#9422-7 *Lounging Luxury.*

#9417-7 *Hidden Glamor.*

Dad's and Ted's Clothes on Cards

9451-6-100	broadcloth shirt (assorted colors), hanger
9452-4-100	slacks (assorted colors), hanger
9453-2-100	Bermuda shorts, high socks, hanger
9456-5-120	pajamas, slippers, hanger
9457-3-120	bathrobe, slippers, hanger
9458-1-120	pullover sweater, hanger
9461-5-120	blazer jacket, hanger
9462-3-150	cardigan sweater, socks, hanger
9463-1-150	vest, tie, shoes, hanger
9466-4-200	sweater, slacks, hanger
9467-2-200	car coat, cap, hanger
9468-0-200	suit jacket and trousers, shoes, hanger

#9463-1 vest.

All of Dad's and Ted's clothes on cards are from the *Betty Ann Snider Collection*.

Above left: #9451-6 shirt.

Above, right: #9452-4 slacks.

Right: #9453-2 Bermuda shorts.

#9461-5 blazer.

#9457-3 bathrobe, slippers.

#9462-3 cardigan sweater, socks.

#9456-5 pajamas, slippers.

#9458-1 pullover sweater.

#9468-0 suit jacket and trousers, shoes.

#9466-4 sweater, slacks.

#9467-2 car coat, cap.

79

Patterns

The following pages show the commercial patterns that were issued to include Tammy dolls. Many of the patterns also say that they fit other pre-teen dolls of 11½ to 12in. *Woman's Day* Magazine of February 1967 showed Tammy, Pepper and Ted in several different outfits and knitted sweaters for which patterns and instructions could be ordered. No credit is given to Ideal on these.

5771

Doll
One Size

Simplicity Printed Pattern 50¢
IN CANADA 60¢

tammy & pepper
Sister Wardrobe

* © Tammy 1962, Pepper 1963, Ideal Toy Corp.   Trademarks Tammy® and Pepper® used under license.

<table>
<tr><td colspan="2">Butterick</td><td colspan="2">Simplicity</td></tr>
<tr><td>2931</td><td>no date</td><td>4883</td><td>no date</td></tr>
<tr><td></td><td></td><td>5214</td><td>no date</td></tr>
<tr><td colspan="2">McCall's</td><td>5446</td><td>© 1964</td></tr>
<tr><td>2123</td><td>© 1969</td><td>5771</td><td>© 1964</td></tr>
<tr><td>6987</td><td>© 1963</td><td>5852</td><td>© 1964</td></tr>
<tr><td>7673</td><td>© 1964</td><td>5859</td><td>© 1964</td></tr>
<tr><td>9099</td><td>© 1967</td><td>5899</td><td>© 1965</td></tr>
<tr><td>9605</td><td>© 1968</td><td>5941</td><td>© 1965</td></tr>
<tr><td></td><td></td><td>6107</td><td>© 1965</td></tr>
<tr><td></td><td></td><td>6150</td><td>© 1965</td></tr>
<tr><td></td><td></td><td>6244</td><td>© 1965</td></tr>
</table>

Most of the patterns are from the *Naomi C. Stroup Collection.*

5859

Girl
Size 8
Breast 26

Simplicity Printed Pattern 50c IN CANADA 60c

an authentic *tammy* fashion for girls and dress-alike clothes for Tammy® doll

® ©1962 IDEAL TOY CORP
TRADEMARK TAMMY® USED UNDER LICENSE

4883

Doll One Size

Simplicity Printed Pattern 50c IN CANADA 60c

5899

Child
Size 6

Simplicity Printed Pattern 50c IN CANADA 60c

Jiffy
authentic *tammy* fashion for girls and dress-alike clothes for Tammy· doll

® ©1962 Ideal Toy Corp., Trademark Tammy ® used under license

5941

CHILD
Size 6

10 BW

Simplicity Printed Pattern 50c IN CANADA 60c

Jiffy
authentic *tammy.* fashion for girls and dress-alike clothes for Tammy· doll

® ©1962 Ideal Toy Corp., Trademark Tammy ® used under license

82

McCall's 2123 Step-by-Step Pattern
TEEN FASHION DOLLS' INSTANT WARDROBE
ONE SIZE—11½" DOLL
65¢
75¢ IN CANADA

FITS:
Barbie
Francie
Casey
Julia
Christie
Midge
Barbara Joe
Babs
Gina
Annette
Batgirl
Mera
Wonder Woman
Supergirl
Betty
Maddie Mod
Tammy
Stacey
and others

McCall's 9605 PRINTED PATTERN
TEEN FASHION DOLLS' INSTANT WARDROBE
ONE SIZE—11½" DOLL
65¢
75¢ IN CANADA

FITS:—Barbie / Francie / Casey / Midge / Barbara Joe / Babs / Gina / Annette / Batgirl / Mera
Wonder Woman / Supergirl / Tammy and others

McCall's 9099 PRINTED PATTERN
TEEN FASHION DOLLS' INSTANT WARDROBE
ONE SIZE—11½" DOLL
50¢
50¢ IN CANADA

FITS:
Barbie
Francie
Casey
Midge
Barbara Joe
Babs
Gina
Annette
Batgirl
Mera
Wonder Woma
Supergirl
Tammy
and others

PRE-TEEN WARDROBE FOR 11½" Betsy McCall Doll
also fits "TAMMY" and other pre-teen dolls 11½"-12"

A B C D E F G H

McCall's #7673.

Books, Paper Dolls, Games, etc.

The Tammy book, *Adventure in Squaw Valley*, is a hardback juvenile novel, published by the Whitman Publishing Company. It was written by Winifred E. Wise and illustrated by Haris Petie and was copyrighted by Ideal Toy Corporation in 1964.

In the same format as the above book is *Adventure in Hollywood*, also copyrighted 1964 by Ideal Toy Corporation. The author is Alice Wellman and it was illustrated by Haris Petie.

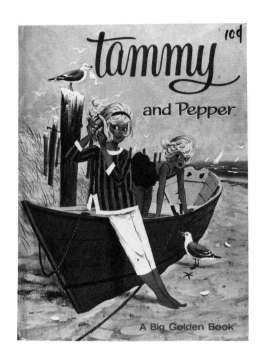

A Big Golden Book (9¹/₂ by 12³/₄in), *Tammy and Pepper*, produced for younger children. The author is Kathryn Hitte and the pictures are by Mel Crawford. This was published by Golden Press and copyright 1964 by Ideal Toy Corporation.

Above right: *Tammy and Her Family* in a small-format coloring book by Whitman, No. 1134, copyright 1964 by Ideal Toy Corporation. This book, as the cover attests, has 128 pages to color.

Tammy and Her Family paper dolls are from a folder, shown on page 88. This is No. 1997 by Whitman, copyright 1964 by Ideal Toy Corporation. This same set was also printed in a smaller size with the dolls on very heavy board and came in the storage box shown on page 90.

Whitman folder No. 1997, for the paper doll set shown on page 87. *Richard Rusnock Collection.*

Tammy's Closet Full of Clothes, Whitman No. 4620, copyright 1965 by Ideal Toy Corporation.

Tammy and Pepper paper doll folder, Whitman No. 1997, copyright 1965 by Ideal Toy Corporation. The paper dolls are on heavy card stock inside the folder.

Tammy and Pepper Paper Doll Activity Book, Golden Press, Inc., No. GF221, copyright 1964, 1963 by Ideal Toy Corp.

Tammy Cut-Out Dolls, Watkins Strathmore Co., No. 1885D, copyright 1963 by Ideal Toy Corporation.

Tammy, a Little Golden Activity Book, No. A52, copyright 1963 by Ideal Toy Corporation. The story is by Kathleen N. Daly with pictures by Ada Salvi. There are ten pages of clothing adapted from the Ideal boxed fashion sets.

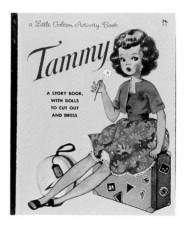

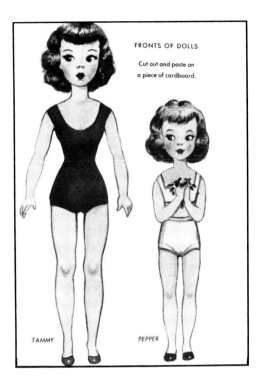

Left: Tammy and Pepper paper dolls from the Little Golden Book shown on page 89.

Below: Advertisement from the 1964 Christmas Catalog. *Courtesy of Sears, Roebuck and Co.* Note how reasonable the original price now seems for all these things.

Tammy and her Family of Dolls $2⁹⁷

Five board dolls . . Tammy and her delightful family—Mom, Dad, sister Pepper and brother Ted, plus a set of beautiful die-cut clothes; Tammy coloring book of 132 pages; Tammy puzzle; magic water-color paint with board plus color picture guide with instructions; magic slate with stylus; magic wipe-off board with 5 magic crayons; plastic scissors; 6 crayons; 8 paints with brush; 4 sewing cards; 4 laces; package of daisy chains; 12-sheets multi-colored paper . . 52 pieces plus 32 pages creative paper. Storage box.
3 N 694—Shipping weight 3 pounds 6 ounces $2.97

Right: Tammy Game from the Christmas catalog, 1964. *Courtesy Montgomery Ward and Co., Inc.*

Tammy Game. 2 to 4 players are dealt 7 cards. Spin spinner and move around board, drawing and discarding until 1 player has 3 cards of a kind and 4 cards of a kind. This gives her a hip-flip card. First player to have 3 hip-flip cards wins. Excitement galore for ages 7 and up.

49 U 432—Wt. 1 lb. 14 oz.....$2.39

Below: The tea set is from the Christmas catalog of 1963. *Courtesy Montgomery Ward and Co., Inc.* The Tammy Tea Set has service for six and includes six metal plates, six saucers, six plastic cups and tumblers, six sets of plastic cutlery, a teapot and cover, a sugar bowl, creamer, and six paper napkins.

[13] "Tammy" Tea Set $3³³

The Tammy Card Game is standard size playing cards and is packaged in a clear plastic case. It is No. 4491 by the Whitman Publishing Co., copyright 1964 by Ideal Toy Corporation.

The Tammy and Pepper Bank Book by Ideal is a plastic bank made like a book. It measures $4^1/_2$ by $6^1/_8$ inches and has sliding panels on the bottom and "page" side for retrieval of the savings. This is item No. 4095-0 and is copyright 1964.

Tammy's Sing-A-Long Party is a 33 1/3 RPM "album" by Little World Records, No. LW-903, copyright 1965 by Ideal Toy Corp. The singing is by a professional group who gets no credit on either the album cover or on the record itself. All of the tunes on this record are ones that would appeal to very young children. The first one, *Tammy T.V. Theme*, is obviously taken from a television commercial for Ideal's Tammy dolls. It begins, "Tammy the ideal teen, she's a doll, she's ideal, she's sweet sixteen." There are six albums in this series and all the covers show Tammy dolls and accessories by Ideal. The other albums in the series are:

> *Meet Tammy & Her Friends*
> *Tammy's Favorite Fairy Tales*
> *Tammy's Big Parade*
> *Tammy in Fairyland*
> *Merry Christmas with Tammy*

Tammy Accessories

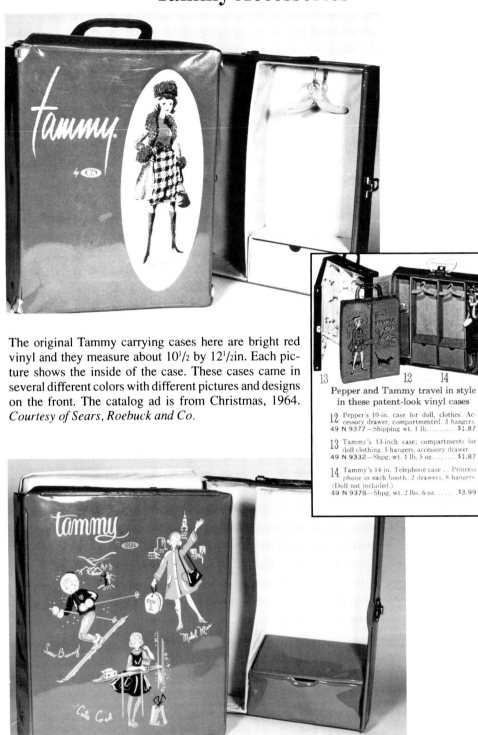

The original Tammy carrying cases here are bright red vinyl and they measure about 10¹/₂ by 12¹/₂in. Each picture shows the inside of the case. These cases came in several different colors with different pictures and designs on the front. The catalog ad is from Christmas, 1964. *Courtesy of Sears, Roebuck and Co.*

13   12   14

Pepper and Tammy travel in style
in these patent-look vinyl cases

12 Pepper's 10-in. case for doll, clothes. Accessory drawer, compartmented. 5 hangers.
49 N 9377—Shipping wt. 1 lb.........$1.87

13 Tammy's 13-inch case; compartments for doll clothing. 5 hangers, accessory drawer.
49 N 9332—Shpg. wt. 1 lb. 5 oz.......$1.87

14 Tammy's 14-in. Telephone case . . Princess phone in each booth. 2 drawers, 8 hangers. (Doll not included.)
49 N 9378—Shpg. wt. 2 lbs. 6 oz......$3.99

Tammy's House, No. 9702-2, is made of heavy lithographed cardboard and was first advertised in 1963. In 1964 Montgomery Ward offered it for $4.99. *Courtesy Montgomery Ward and Co., Inc.* The house with furniture, also made of heavy cardboard, folds up and when open it measures about 43in wide, 34in deep and 15in high. *Betty Ann Snider Collection. Top photograph by Phillip M. Snider.*

Pepper's Tree House. The box is copyright 1965 and is No. 9712-1 from Ideal. The tree house is 32in tall and is made of plastic with lithographed cardboard for the "foliage." The set includes all sorts of accessories and furniture and is shown in a complete view on the opposite page. In the 1965 Sears Christmas Catalog this sold for $6.97; the General Merchandise Company Catalog of the same year offered it for $8.98. The original box shown here was priced $7.99 by Montgomery Ward and was marked down to $4.99. The Pepper doll is New Pepper wearing outfit #9318-7, *After School*, with the hooded pullover that has her name on it. The boys are Pos'n Pete in two different original outfits. *Lee Jenkins Collection.*

PEPPER'S PONY by Ideal. Fun on the gallop, as imaginations race cross-country with Pepper's new pony! Sized just right for Pepper and friends, this frisky realistic steed is brown and white; comes with fine-detailed plastic saddle and bridle. And his box is his very own stall!

980V086 F188
Wt. 1½ lbs.....**$2.98**

630

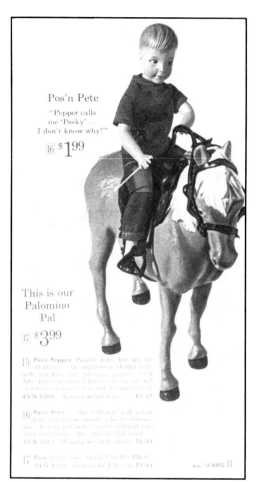

Pos'n Pete

"Pepper calls me 'Pesky'.. I don't know why!"

16 $ 1 99

This is our Palomino Pal

17 $ 3 99

15 Pos'n Pepper. Posable arms, legs act out all games... she's outfitted in pleated skirt with matching knit earrings, panties, and date. Luxurious rooted hair can be set and styled over and over. Vinyl, 9 in. tall in undies box!
49-N 3309... shipping weight 8 oz..... $2.37

16 Pos'n Pete... the realistic boy with action joints that move, stands, sits, or crouches in jeans, patched knit sweater and knit polo shirt, vinyl boots. Plastic 9 in. tall, vinyl.
49-N 3312... shipping weight 8 oz..... $1.99

17 Pony-Saddle. Soft Saddle. Detailed Plastic
49-N 3375... shipping wt. 1 lb. 8 oz. $3.99

SEARS 31

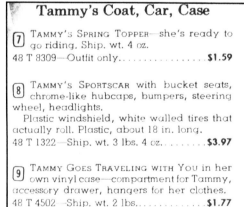

Tammy's Coat, Car, Case

7 TAMMY'S SPRING TOPPER—she's ready to go riding. Ship. wt. 4 oz.
48 T 8309—Outfit only.................**$1.59**

8 TAMMY'S SPORTSCAR with bucket seats, chrome-like hubcaps, bumpers, steering wheel, headlights.
   Plastic windshield, white walled tires that actually roll. Plastic, about 18 in. long.
48 T 1322—Ship. wt. 3 lbs. 4 oz........**$3.97**

9 TAMMY GOES TRAVELING WITH YOU in her own vinyl case—compartment for Tammy, accessory drawer, hangers for her clothes.
48 T 4502—Ship. wt. 2 lbs..............**$1.77**

This page shows some rare Tammy items that have not been found in original condition. Pete's Palomino Pal is from the Christmas Catalog of 1964. *Courtesy of Sears, Roebuck and Co.*; Pepper's Pony was advertised by the General Merchandise Co. in 1965; Tammy's car is from the Christmas catalog of 1964. *Courtesy Montgomery Ward and Co., Inc.*

Wind-up Juke Boxes made of plastic. Pepper's Juke Box, Ideal No. 9717-0 dated 1965, is about 7in high and it plays "Music, Music, Music." *Betty Ann Snider Collection. Photograph by Phillip M. Snider.* Tammy's Juke Box is from the 1964 Christmas Catalog. *Courtesy of Sears, Roebuck and Co.*

This ad for Tammy's Boat is from the 1963 Ideal Catalog.

The Tammy and Ted Catamaran is Ideal No. 9706-5 from 1964 and is 18 inches long and 23 inches high. *Betty Ann Snider Collection. Photograph by Phillip M. Snider.*

Tammy's bedroom furniture was advertised in 1964 in the Christmas catalogs of Montgomery Ward, Sears and Spiegel. The catalog ad below is *courtesy of Sears, Roebuck and Co.* Above is Pos'n Tammy sitting on her original bed. The bed has no markings on it but it is of the same type and construction as the Strombecker wooden furniture made for other dolls, like Vogue's Ginny.

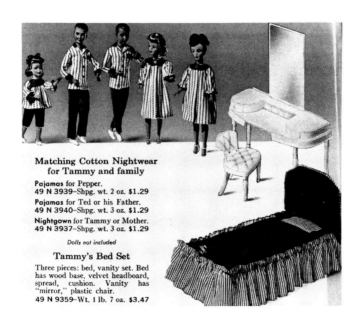

Matching Cotton Nightwear for Tammy and family

Pajamas for Pepper.
49 N 3939–Shpg. wt. 2 oz. $1.29
Pajamas for Ted or his Father.
49 N 3940–Shpg. wt. 3 oz. $1.29
Nightgown for Tammy or Mother.
49 N 3937–Shpg. wt. 3 oz. $1.29

Dolls not included

Tammy's Bed Set

Three pieces: bed, vanity set. Bed has wood base, velvet headboard, spread, cushion. Vanity has "mirror," plastic chair.
49 N 9359–Wt. 1 lb. 7 oz. $3.47

Tammy-Type Dolls

Many imitators of the Tammy doll were on the market shortly after Tammy was first produced in 1962. Some of these dolls are well modeled and well made; others are dolls that were manufactured to sell at a lower cost.

The black Tammy-type is 11¼in tall and has a beautifully molded head with black rooted hair but the body is made of plastic that is crudely finished and is only marked MADE IN // HONG KONG. The blonde is 12in tall with rooted hair and the head is marked: "©//UNIQUE."

Another Tammy look-alike is the 11³/₄in doll with a similar head marked: "© EEGEE." The plastic body also shows mold marks at the seams. The ring in the center of the doll's back pulls the long strand of hair inside of the head and a tug on the hair makes it "grow" again. *Dori O'Melia Collection.*

This doll is marked UNIQUE like the blonde doll on page 102. She is dressed in her original outfit to represent *Elly May Clampett* from the television series "The Beverly Hillbillies" (CBS — September 26, 1962 to September 7, 1971). She is 12in tall.

A variation of the UNIQUE marked doll on the opposite page is *Calico Lass*, who was a premium offered by Kellogg's Cereal (Patricia R. Smith: *Teen Dolls*, Collector Books, 1977). The smaller doll is her "sister" and she is 9¼in tall with rooted blonde hair and a body that retains the mold marks at the seams and is similar to the Dodi body by Ideal. Her head is marked: "UNIQUE // 19©65." *Dori O'Melia Collection.*

Walt Disney's Cinderella Doll

12-inch doll dressed elegantly for the ball, in pink

$7⁴⁴

$3⁹⁴

Samantha . . the Witch

Dolls from the Christmas Catalog of 1965. *Courtesy of Sears, Roebuck and Co.* The *Walt Disney's Cinderella* had an extra head with long straight hair. The maker is unknown. *Samantha the Witch* represented Elizabeth Montgomery from the television show "Bewitched" (ABC — September 17, 1964 to July 1, 1972). She is also 12in tall and was made by Ideal, using the construction of the Grown-Up Pos'n Tammy. Movie and television star *Patty Duke* was made by Horsman.

Patty Duke Teen Doll
$2⁹⁷

You can tell she's a teen-age doll
. . she has her own phone. She's 12
inches of vinyl plastic with Super-
flex arms and legs that bend, pose
in teen-age manner. Rooted hair.
49 N 3881—Wt. 12 oz....$2.97

Teenage SUZY
with 4 daytime outfits $2⁹⁹

Suzy is 12 inches tall. Has rooted hair in a popular teen-age style. Dressed in colorful sunsuit. Other outfits include: 2-piece culotte ensemble; cotton dress, sleeveless dress, 2-piece knit suit. Purse, shoes. Vinyl head; jointed plastic body.

49 N 3834—Shipping weight 8 oz.... $2.99

9-inch PEGGY Doll
with casual wardrobe $2⁹⁹

This little girl has rooted hair. She's dressed in a sporty sunsuit. 4 extra outfits: blue jeans, checked sleeveless blouse; felt weskit with skirt; coat; housecoat. Other accessories: panties, hangers, purse, belt, comb. Vinyl head, jointed plastic body.

49 N 3831—Shipping weight 6 oz.... $2.99

A catalog ad from Christmas of 1964 for *Suzy* and *Peggy* shows that there was a market for lower priced imitators of Tammy and Pepper with ready-made wardrobes. *Courtesy of Sears, Roebuck and Co.* The various Christmas catalogs from 1963 to 1966 showed different dolls that were similar to Tammy and Pepper and also offered various outfits for them that were close in design to the genuine Ideal boxed sets.

Walt Disney's *Mary Poppins* represents Julie Andrews in her
1964 Academy Award winning role. (Julie Andrews' name was
not used for this doll or for *The Sound of Music* doll by Madame
Alexander.) The Mary Poppins doll came out in 1964. The catalog ad is from Christmas of 1965. *Courtesy of Sears, Roebuck
and Co.*, and shows the extra costumes, modeled by the two
dolls on the opposite page. These dolls are by Horsman and have
painted blue eyes, rooted dark brown hair and red lips. The only
marking is on the head: H. (Some have a 2 incised on the lower
back also.) The version in the original box dates from about 1973.
The only difference in this doll and the earlier ones is that the
lips are painted pink, the clothing is much simpler in design and
the umbrella is only cardboard. This doll was designed by Irene
Szor and is Style No. 928. All of the Mary Poppins dolls measure $11\frac{1}{2}$in.

The film *The Blue Bird* was released by Twentieth Century-Fox in 1976 and was the first co-production between the United States and the Soviet Union. The star-studded cast was headed by Elizabeth Taylor, Jane Fonda, Ava Gardner and Cicely Tyson but the film could be summed up in one word: Boring. It was such a flop that it was not widely distributed. Fox should have learned its lesson and avoided re-filming the Maurice Maeterlinck fairy tale. In 1940 Twentieth Century-Fox filmed *The Blue Bird* with Shirley Temple and it was her first big failure.

The Elizabeth Taylor is the exact same doll as the Mary Poppins and was also designed by Irene Szor. She is Style No. 9921, copyright 1976 by Twentieth Century-Fox Film Corporation. Above is the original package with the extra costumes, all of which are very simply and economically made. The doll was no more successful than the movie and was quickly remaindered. Its one noteworthy feature was that it was made in the United States, unlike most of the dolls at that time, which were made in the Far East.

Above: A Penny Brite folder, which shows her extra clothing and accessories.

Right: Penny Brite in her plastic carrying case, the original packaging.

Perhaps the most charming of all the dolls that came out after the success of Tammy and Pepper is *Penny Brite* by Deluxe Reading Corporation in 1964. Penny Brite dolls measure $8^{1}/_{8}$ to $8^{1}/_{2}$in tall. They have blonde rooted hair of various lengths; painted eyes are black and the open/closed mouth has painted teeth. There is wire inside the vinyl arms and legs for bending Penny Brite into different positions. The plastic torso is marked on the back:

DELUXE READING CORP.
ELIZABETH, N.J.
PAT. PENDING

The head is incised:

A-9
8132
DELUXE READING CORP.
© 1963

The second line can also be: A100 or B143 or is blank.

Two of the Penny Brites above are wearing the original dress from the basic doll which was sold in the plastic carrying case on the opposite page.

EXTRA PACKAGED
PENNY BRITE OUTFITS

Chit Chat	black velvet pants, white printed top, black bow, red shoes, telephone, date book, hanger
Singing in the Rain	raincoat, hat, umbrella, boots, hanger
Fun in the Sun	bathing suit, robe, sandals, towel, sunglasses, hanger
Winter Princess	stretch pants, sweater, hat, ice skates, hanger
Anchors Aweigh	navy suit, matching sailor hat, purse, shoes, hanger
Flower Girl	formal, shoes, bouquet, bow, hanger

One of the Penny Brite boxed play sets is shown at right from a Penny Brite folder. The other sets were:

Kitchen Dinette	with furniture and clothing
Travel Set	with car, luggage, dog and coat set
Beauty Parlour	with furniture and smock
Bedroom Set	with furniture and pajamas

Complete set fully assembled ready for play—in this beautifully illustrated take-home package.

SCHOOLROOM—Penny Brite learns her ABC's like a real little girl. • Desk and Chair—modern as today's newest schoolroom. • Blackboard and Easel is a real one... with chalk and eraser. • Briefcase realistically designed ... there's also a pen and book. • Includes simulated Penny Brite Doll* wearing actual Penny Brite 2-piece schoolgirl dress. *Penny Brite Doll is sold separately in her combination wardrobe-carrying case.

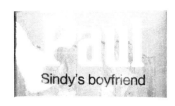
Sindy's boyfriend

Above is the folder showing all the extra costumes for Sindy and Paul from New Zealand by Lines Brothers, under license from Pedigree. At the right and below are their original boxes.

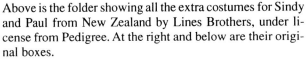

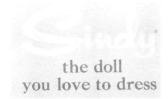
the doll you love to dress

Sindy by Pedigree of England was introduced in 1963 as "the doll you love to dress," using the same advertising approach as Ideal had for Tammy. Sindy at first was jointed like Tammy and she gradually became more articulated over the years, with bending knees, ankles, elbows and with extra joints at the waist and the wrists. She was also marketed in Australia and the United States by Pedigree. In New Zealand she was made by Lines Brothers Limited under license from Pedigree. Sindy, who was 11$\frac{1}{2}$in tall, had a "family" of dolls. Her boyfriend Paul was 12in tall; her "English girlfriend Vicki" and her "continental girlfriend Mitzi" were 11$\frac{3}{4}$in tall and had fixed waists; her little sister Patch and Patch's friend Poppet were 9in tall. All of the dolls had extensive wardrobes and accessories. Sindy was even more typical of her era than Tammy was, as her costumes bore a strong resemblance to the contemporary designs of Mary Quant, London's leading fashion designer of the 1960s. Paul's outfits looked like the clothes that the Beatles wore when they first became famous in 1964.

The two dolls pictured are early dolls from the Pedigree series and were made in New Zealand. Sindy is 11½in tall and has painted blue eyes and rooted dark brown hair. The original box calls her basic outfit "Sindy in Weekenders." Her arms and legs have wire inside for posing her in different positions. The doll is not marked but the box says "Made in New Zealand by Lines Bros. (N.Z.) Ltd." The plastic stand is marked: PEDIGREE NZ

Paul is 12in tall with painted brown hair and painted olive green eyes. His legs and arms also bend for posing (note the similarity to the hands of Bud, page 20). Like Sindy, Paul is not marked, but the box and the stand are marked like Sindy's. *Dori O'Melia Collection.*

Left: Sindy #12GSS Blonde. This costume was called *Honalulu Holiday* [sic] and the box also included the weekenders shown on Sindy on page 115. This doll with her rooted blonde hair shows even more clearly how similar the doll is to Tammy. She also has bending legs and arms. The box tells that the doll was "made in Hong Kong for Pedigree Dolls Limited." The doll is again unmarked but the stand is incised: PEDIGREE // MADE IN HONG KONG. *Dori O'Melia Collection.*

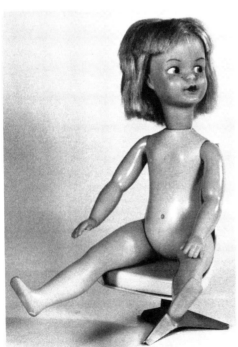

Lower left: 9in Patch, Sindy's little sister, is unmarked. She has soft rooted blonde hair and freckles across her nose and has wire in the arms and legs for posing. The entire doll is like Ideal's Pepper. Patch was made by Lines Brothers, distributors of the Pedigree dolls, who have since gone out of business. *Dori O'Melia Collection.*

Below: From "The Sindy Set" booklet, showing that Sindy, like Tammy and Her Family, had many other accessories, such as beds and wardrobes for their clothing.

Sindy's Car
Sindy's the envy of all her friends because she's got every grown-up girl's dream: a red two-seater sports car! It's perfect in every detail with chrome bumpers, hub-caps and headlamps. Finished dashboard and sleek wide windscreen. Radio aerial has Sindy banner to flutter in the breeze. **12SA1.**
Not Available in Australia

Sindy's Horse
At the local gymkhana and for morning canters, Sindy rides high on her very own horse which comes complete with saddle, bridle, stirrups and is a real champion. **12SA4.** *Available later. Not Available in Australia*

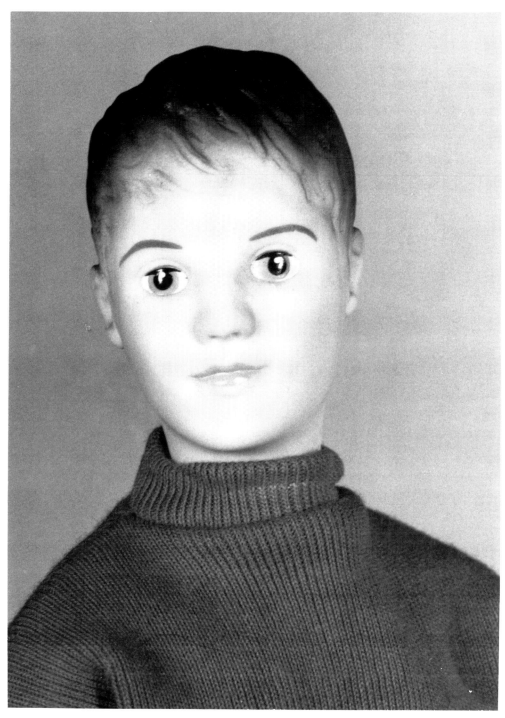

Paul made by Lines Brothers in New Zealand.

Sleep-eyed Sindy. She has dark brown rooted hair and dark blue side-glancing eyes. This is *Sweet Dreams*, #44694. The doll is 11in tall and is marked on the head:

033390

54

The lover back is marked: HONG KONG
Dori O'Melia Collection.

Royal Occassion, #44659. Sindy has blue painted eyes and dark blonde rooted hair. The doll is not marked; the dress tag reads: MADE IN HONG KONG. *Dori O'Melia Collection.*

119

The fashions that put Sindy ahead
New designs to excite collectors
Fine finish and attention to detail

Out and about fashions

44320 Winter Nights.
Long nylon nightdress and yellow towelling hooded dressing gown. Both trimmed with embroidered braid.

44322 Seaside Special.
Towelling bikini with wrap around beach skirt, and stretch towelling beach jacket with lined hood. Matching beach bag

44321 Tartan Touch.
Elegant tartan evening dress with frilled lace trimmed hem. Lace shawl and evening bag

On this page and opposite is a two-page spread from the 1979 Pedigree catalog show-ing some of the extra fashions available for Sindy.

44323 Country Club.
Cream pleated skirt with double
breasted tailored jacket and
gingham blouse. Brown nylon
beret.

44324 Rainy Days.
Belted navy blue gabardine
raincoat has hood with striped
lining and matching cuff trim.
Complete with shoulder bag and
red scarf.

Scenesetters

Some of the accessories available for
Pedigree's Sindy in 1979 are shown at the
right in a folder that came with the dolls im-
ported from England.

121

Sindy with a line of furniture was made for distribution in the United States by Louis Marx & Co., Inc. in the late 1970s. Sindy is 11 in tall with rooted hair and painted eyes. She is fully-jointed and poseable with extra joints at the waist and the wrists. Two versions of the doll were available - Sindy, with blonde rooted hair, and Sindy's Friend, with black rooted hair. Both dolls are marked on the head:

2 GEN 1077

033055X

The back is marked below the jointed waist:

MADE IN

HONG KONG

At the left is Sindy's Friend. Below is Sindy serving dinner to her in the Marx *Scenesetter* #1601. (See page 121 for the similar room display by Pedigree.) The furniture is Dining Table and Chairs with Dinnerware, #1235, and Breakfront with Desert Service, #1236.

Marx Toys Sindy. Note the arms bent at the elbows.
They have wires inside like Pos'n Tammy and other
dolls in Her Family.

Price Guide

The "prices" for collectibles that pertain to the Tammy dolls and related items are not meant to be absolutes; they are suggestions based on current values from doll shows, advertisements and mailing lists.

The price range, for example $60-75; 90 MIB, covers an item that is in good condition to one that is in excellent condition; MIB refers to unplayed-with and still "Mint in Box."

Tammy and Her Family of Dolls

Bud	$60-75	90 MIB *RARE*
Dad	$20-40	50 MIB
Dodi (from 1960s)	$20-35	45+MIB
Glamour Misty	$30-50	70+MIB
Pos'n Misty	$20-35	60 MIB
Pos'n Misty with Phone Booth	$30-50	60+MIB
Mom	$20-40	50 MIB
Patti	$30-50	60-80 MIB *RARE*
Pepper		
1963; 1964 Pepper	$20-30	45 MIB
Ideal of Canada	$15-25	35 MIB
New Pepper	$20-25	35 MIB
Pos'n Pepper	$20-30	30-45 MIB
Pete	$25-40	50-60 MIB
Salty	$30-45	55-75 MIB *RARE*
Suntan Dodi	$10-20	25-30 MIB
Tammy:		
Black (Grown Up)	$40-55	60-80 MIB
First Issue*	$15-25	30-50 MIB
Grown-Up	$15-25	35 MIB
Grown Up Pos'n	$15-25	35 MIB
Ideal of Canada	$20-30	30-40 MIB
Pos'n	$25-35	50 MIB
Reliable (Canada)	$20-30	45 MIB
with Phone Booth	$30-50	60 MIB
Ted	$30-40	50 MIB
Pos'n Ted	$25-35	30-40 MIB

*Blonde hair is more common than dark hair.

Clothing for Tammy Family

(Prices are for complete packages that are still intact on card or in box.)

Tammy on cards . . . . $ 8-20

Tammy in boxes

    Numbers that end in 150
    (for example, 9051-4-150) $20-30

    Numbers that end in 200 . . . . $20-30

    Numbers that end in 250 . . . . $20-30

    Numbers that end in 300 . . . . $30-40

    Numbers that end in 350 . . . . $30-45

    Numbers that end in 400 . . . . $30-45

    Numbers that end in 500 . . . . $35-45

Tammy in Canadian packages $30-45

Pepper on cards $15-25

Pepper boxes sets (also Dodi) $25-35

Mom on cards $15-25

Dad and Ted on cards $20-35

Other Tammy Collectibles

Bed, complete with "Tammy"
    printed on spread $30-60

Boat or Catamaran with "Tammy"
    printed on sail . . . . $45-75 *RARE*

Books, hardback with "Tammy"
    in the title . . . . $ 5-15

Car designed for Tammy $20-35

Cases for dolls with "Tammy"
    printed on the front $15-25

Coloring books (uncolored) $10-25

Doll House $45-65

Games $15-25

Juke Box for Tammy or Pepper . . . . . . $35-50 *RARE*

Little Golden Book (Tammy) $35-45

Paper doll booklets (uncut) $20-45

Paper doll sets boxed and complete . . . $20-50

Patterns . . . . $ 4-10

Phone Booth (without doll) $12-18

Pony (markings not known) . . . .   ?   *RARE*

Tea Set $20-35

Tree House (Pepper) $60-75

Tammy-types and Similar Dolls

Calico Lass	$15-25	30-40 MIB
(if dressed in original outfit)		
Eegee	$25-30	
Elizabeth Taylor	$30-50	50-75 MIB
Elly May Clampett	$20-30	35-50 MIB
(if dressed in original outfit)		
Grant Plastics	$10-15	
Mary Poppins (1964)	$20-35	40-50 MIB
Mary Poppins (1973)	$15-20	25 MIB
Mitzi (Pedigree)	$25-50	
Patch	$30-45	
Patty Duke	$35-55	60 MIB
Paul	$35-45	55 MIB
Penny Brite	$10-15	15-25 MIB
Poppet	$25-40	
Samantha, the Witch	$80-100	100-150 MIB
Sindy (Marx)	$20-25	30 MIB
Sindy (Pedigree)		
early version, not fully jointed	$20-35	40 MIB
later versions, fully jointed	$10-20	
Sindy's Friend (Marx)	$30-40	50 MIB
Susi (Brazil)	$20-35	40 MIB
Unique	$20-30	
Unique "little sister"	$20-30	
Vicki (Pedigree)	$25-45	50 MIB
Walt Disney's Cinderella	$60-70	75-100 MIB
Unmarked Tammy-types or marked AE	$10-15	
Unmarked Tammy-types in black versions	$15-20	

Index

(of illustrated items)

About the Author

For more than 20 years John Axe has written research articles on dolls, teddy bears and other collectibles for various magazines. He is also an award-winning paper doll artist whose work has been used for Convention Souvenirs, as well as having been published in book form.

John is very active with the United Federation of Doll Clubs, Inc. He was the first Chairman of the Modern (Doll) Competitive Exhibit and has been Chairman of Judges (Modern) several times. He is a past editor of *Doll News*, the journal of UFDC.

In 1990 John was awarded with the Excellence in Research and Writing Award from the International Doll Academy and in 1992 with the UFDC Award of Excellence for Contributions to *Doll News*.

John also designs teddy bears for Merrythought Limited and in 1989 was awarded with a Golden Teddy Award for his bear Jeremy.

Other books by John Axe

- *Collectible Boy Dolls*
- *Collectible Dolls in National Costume*
- *The Collectible Dionne Quintuplets*
- *Collectible Black Dolls*
- *Collectible Patsy Dolls and Patsy-Types*
- *Collectible Sonja Henie*
- *Tammy and Dolls You Love to Dress*
- *The Encyclopedia of Celebrity Dolls*
- *Effanbee: A Collector's Encyclopedia 1949-1983*
- *Celebrity Doll Price Guide and Annual*
  (with A. Glenn Mandeville)
- *The Magic of Merrythought*
- *Kewpies — Dolls & Art of Rose O'Neill and Joseph L. Kallus*
- *Romantic Heroes of Fiction Paper Dolls*
- *Royal Children Paper Dolls: Queen Victoria to Queen Elizabeth II*
- *The Best of John Axe*
- *Effanbee: A Collector's Encyclopedia 1949-Present*